Password Keeper

Save Passwords • Wi-Fi Log Ins • Software Licenses

A Simple Start Guide

Password Keeper
Published by Simple Start Guides
Everett, WA 98201

SimpleStartGuides@gmail.com

Cover photograph by Cindy Shebley

ISBN: 9781794321601

A

Website/Account	
User Name	
Password	
Website URL	
Notes	

Website/Account	
User Name	
Password	
Website URL	
Notes	

Website/Account	
User Name	
Password	
Website URL	
Notes	

Website/Account	
User Name	
Password	
Website URL	
Notes	

A PASSWORDS and LOG-INS

Website/Account	
User Name	
Password	
Website URL	
Notes	

Website/Account	
User Name	
Password	
Website URL	
Notes	

Website/Account	
User Name	
Password	
Website URL	
Notes	

Website/Account	
User Name	
Password	
Website URL	
Notes	

Website/Account	
User Name	
Password	
Website URL	
Notes	

Website/Account	
User Name	
Password	
Website URL	
Notes	

Website/Account	
User Name	
Password	
Website URL	
Notes	

Website/Account	
User Name	
Password	
Website URL	
Notes	

PASSWORDS and LOG-INS

Website/Account	
User Name	
Password	
Website URL	
Notes	

Website/Account	
User Name	
Password	
Website URL	
Notes	

Website/Account	
User Name	
Password	
Website URL	
Notes	

Website/Account	
User Name	
Password	
Website URL	
Notes	

Website/Account	
User Name	
Password	
Website URL	
Notes	

Website/Account	
User Name	
Password	
Website URL	
Notes	

Website/Account	
User Name	
Password	
Website URL	
Notes	

Website/Account	
User Name	
Password	
Website URL	
Notes	

Website/Account	
User Name	
Password	
Website URL	
Notes	

Website/Account	
User Name	
Password	
Website URL	
Notes	

Website/Account	
User Name	
Password	
Website URL	
Notes	

Website/Account	
User Name	
Password	
Website URL	
Notes	

B

Website/Account	
User Name	
Password	
Website URL	
Notes	

Website/Account	
User Name	
Password	
Website URL	
Notes	

Website/Account	
User Name	
Password	
Website URL	
Notes	

Website/Account	
User Name	
Password	
Website URL	
Notes	

Website/Account	
User Name	
Password	
Website URL	
Notes	

Website/Account	
User Name	
Password	
Website URL	
Notes	

Website/Account	
User Name	
Password	
Website URL	
Notes	

Website/Account	
User Name	
Password	
Website URL	
Notes	

Website/Account	
User Name	
Password	
Website URL	
Notes	

Website/Account	
User Name	
Password	
Website URL	
Notes	

Website/Account	
User Name	
Password	
Website URL	
Notes	

Website/Account	
User Name	
Password	
Website URL	
Notes	

PASSWORDS and LOG-INS

Website/Account	
User Name	
Password	
Website URL	

Notes

Website/Account	
User Name	
Password	
Website URL	

Notes

Website/Account	
User Name	
Password	
Website URL	

Notes

Website/Account	
User Name	
Password	
Website URL	

Notes

PASSWORDS and LOG-INS

Website/Account	
User Name	
Password	
Website URL	
Notes	

Website/Account	
User Name	
Password	
Website URL	
Notes	

Website/Account	
User Name	
Password	
Website URL	
Notes	

Website/Account	
User Name	
Password	
Website URL	
Notes	

Website/Account	
User Name	
Password	
Website URL	
Notes	

Website/Account	
User Name	
Password	
Website URL	
Notes	

Website/Account	
User Name	
Password	
Website URL	
Notes	

Website/Account	
User Name	
Password	
Website URL	
Notes	

PASSWORDS and LOGINS

Website/Account	
User Name	
Password	
Website URL	
Notes	

Website/Account	
User Name	
Password	
Website URL	
Notes	

Website/Account	
User Name	
Password	
Website URL	
Notes	

Website/Account	
User Name	
Password	
Website URL	
Notes	

Website/Account	
User Name	
Password	
Website URL	
Notes	

Website/Account	
User Name	
Password	
Website URL	
Notes	

Website/Account	
User Name	
Password	
Website URL	
Notes	

Website/Account	
User Name	
Password	
Website URL	
Notes	

Website/Account	
User Name	
Password	
Website URL	
Notes	

Website/Account	
User Name	
Password	
Website URL	
Notes	

Website/Account	
User Name	
Password	
Website URL	
Notes	

Website/Account	
User Name	
Password	
Website URL	
Notes	

Website/Account	
User Name	
Password	
Website URL	
Notes	

Website/Account	
User Name	
Password	
Website URL	
Notes	

Website/Account	
User Name	
Password	
Website URL	
Notes	

Website/Account	
User Name	
Password	
Website URL	
Notes	

Website/Account	
User Name	
Password	
Website URL	
Notes	

Website/Account	
User Name	
Password	
Website URL	
Notes	

Website/Account	
User Name	
Password	
Website URL	
Notes	

Website/Account	
User Name	
Password	
Website URL	
Notes	

Website/Account	
User Name	
Password	
Website URL	
Notes	

Website/Account	
User Name	
Password	
Website URL	
Notes	

Website/Account	
User Name	
Password	
Website URL	
Notes	

Website/Account	
User Name	
Password	
Website URL	
Notes	

Website/Account	
User Name	
Password	
Website URL	
Notes	

Website/Account	
User Name	
Password	
Website URL	
Notes	

Website/Account	
User Name	
Password	
Website URL	
Notes	

Website/Account	
User Name	
Password	
Website URL	
Notes	

Website/Account	
User Name	
Password	
Website URL	
Notes	

Website/Account	
User Name	
Password	
Website URL	
Notes	

Website/Account	
User Name	
Password	
Website URL	
Notes	

Website/Account	
User Name	
Password	
Website URL	
Notes	

PASSWORDS and LOG-INS

E

Website/Account	
User Name	
Password	
Website URL	
Notes	

Website/Account	
User Name	
Password	
Website URL	
Notes	

Website/Account	
User Name	
Password	
Website URL	
Notes	

Website/Account	
User Name	
Password	
Website URL	
Notes	

Website/Account	
User Name	
Password	
Website URL	
Notes	

Website/Account	
User Name	
Password	
Website URL	
Notes	

Website/Account	
User Name	
Password	
Website URL	
Notes	

Website/Account	
User Name	
Password	
Website URL	
Notes	

Website/Account	
User Name	
Password	
Website URL	
Notes	

Website/Account	
User Name	
Password	
Website URL	
Notes	

Website/Account	
User Name	
Password	
Website URL	
Notes	

Website/Account	
User Name	
Password	
Website URL	
Notes	

Website/Account	
User Name	
Password	
Website URL	
Notes	

Website/Account	
User Name	
Password	
Website URL	
Notes	

Website/Account	
User Name	
Password	
Website URL	
Notes	

Website/Account	
User Name	
Password	
Website URL	
Notes	

PASSWORDS and LOGINS F

Website/Account	
User Name	
Password	
Website URL	
Notes	

Website/Account	
User Name	
Password	
Website URL	
Notes	

Website/Account	
User Name	
Password	
Website URL	
Notes	

Website/Account	
User Name	
Password	
Website URL	
Notes	

Website/Account	
User Name	
Password	
Website URL	
Notes	

Website/Account	
User Name	
Password	
Website URL	
Notes	

Website/Account	
User Name	
Password	
Website URL	
Notes	

Website/Account	
User Name	
Password	
Website URL	
Notes	

Website/Account	
User Name	
Password	
Website URL	
Notes	

Website/Account	
User Name	
Password	
Website URL	
Notes	

Website/Account	
User Name	
Password	
Website URL	
Notes	

Website/Account	
User Name	
Password	
Website URL	
Notes	

PASSWORDS and LOG-INS

Website/Account	
User Name	
Password	
Website URL	

Notes

Website/Account	
User Name	
Password	
Website URL	

Notes

Website/Account	
User Name	
Password	
Website URL	

Notes

Website/Account	
User Name	
Password	
Website URL	

Notes

Website/Account	
User Name	
Password	
Website URL	
Notes	

Website/Account	
User Name	
Password	
Website URL	
Notes	

Website/Account	
User Name	
Password	
Website URL	
Notes	

Website/Account	
User Name	
Password	
Website URL	
Notes	

Website/Account	
User Name	
Password	
Website URL	
Notes	

Website/Account	
User Name	
Password	
Website URL	
Notes	

Website/Account	
User Name	
Password	
Website URL	
Notes	

Website/Account	
User Name	
Password	
Website URL	
Notes	

Website/Account	
User Name	
Password	
Website URL	
Notes	

Website/Account	
User Name	
Password	
Website URL	
Notes	

Website/Account	
User Name	
Password	
Website URL	
Notes	

Website/Account	
User Name	
Password	
Website URL	
Notes	

Website/Account	
User Name	
Password	
Website URL	
Notes	

Website/Account	
User Name	
Password	
Website URL	
Notes	

Website/Account	
User Name	
Password	
Website URL	
Notes	

Website/Account	
User Name	
Password	
Website URL	
Notes	

H

Website/Account	
User Name	
Password	
Website URL	
Notes	

Website/Account	
User Name	
Password	
Website URL	
Notes	

Website/Account	
User Name	
Password	
Website URL	
Notes	

Website/Account	
User Name	
Password	
Website URL	
Notes	

PASSWORDS and LOG-INS

Website/Account	
User Name	
Password	
Website URL	
Notes	

Website/Account	
User Name	
Password	
Website URL	
Notes	

Website/Account	
User Name	
Password	
Website URL	
Notes	

Website/Account	
User Name	
Password	
Website URL	
Notes	

Website/Account	
User Name	
Password	
Website URL	
Notes	

Website/Account	
User Name	
Password	
Website URL	
Notes	

Website/Account	
User Name	
Password	
Website URL	
Notes	

Website/Account	
User Name	
Password	
Website URL	
Notes	

PASSWORDS and LOG-INS

Website/Account	
User Name	
Password	
Website URL	
Notes	

Website/Account	
User Name	
Password	
Website URL	
Notes	

Website/Account	
User Name	
Password	
Website URL	
Notes	

Website/Account	
User Name	
Password	
Website URL	
Notes	

PASSWORDS and LOG-INS

Website/Account	
User Name	
Password	
Website URL	
Notes	

Website/Account	
User Name	
Password	
Website URL	
Notes	

Website/Account	
User Name	
Password	
Website URL	
Notes	

Website/Account	
User Name	
Password	
Website URL	
Notes	

PASSWORDS and LOG-INS

Website/Account	
User Name	
Password	
Website URL	
Notes	

Website/Account	
User Name	
Password	
Website URL	
Notes	

Website/Account	
User Name	
Password	
Website URL	
Notes	

Website/Account	
User Name	
Password	
Website URL	
Notes	

PASSWORDS and LOGINS

Website/Account	
User Name	
Password	
Website URL	
Notes	

Website/Account	
User Name	
Password	
Website URL	
Notes	

Website/Account	
User Name	
Password	
Website URL	
Notes	

Website/Account	
User Name	
Password	
Website URL	
Notes	

Website/Account	
User Name	
Password	
Website URL	
Notes	

Website/Account	
User Name	
Password	
Website URL	
Notes	

Website/Account	
User Name	
Password	
Website URL	
Notes	

Website/Account	
User Name	
Password	
Website URL	
Notes	

Website/Account	
User Name	
Password	
Website URL	
Notes	

Website/Account	
User Name	
Password	
Website URL	
Notes	

Website/Account	
User Name	
Password	
Website URL	
Notes	

Website/Account	
User Name	
Password	
Website URL	
Notes	

PASSWORDS and LOG-INS

Website/Account	
User Name	
Password	
Website URL	
Notes	

Website/Account	
User Name	
Password	
Website URL	
Notes	

Website/Account	
User Name	
Password	
Website URL	
Notes	

Website/Account	
User Name	
Password	
Website URL	
Notes	

Website/Account	
User Name	
Password	
Website URL	
Notes	

Website/Account	
User Name	
Password	
Website URL	
Notes	

Website/Account	
User Name	
Password	
Website URL	
Notes	

Website/Account	
User Name	
Password	
Website URL	
Notes	

PASSWORDS and LOG-INS

Website/Account	
User Name	
Password	
Website URL	

Notes

Website/Account	
User Name	
Password	
Website URL	

Notes

Website/Account	
User Name	
Password	
Website URL	

Notes

Website/Account	
User Name	
Password	
Website URL	

Notes

PASSWORDS and LOG-INS

K

Website/Account	
User Name	
Password	
Website URL	
Notes	

Website/Account	
User Name	
Password	
Website URL	
Notes	

Website/Account	
User Name	
Password	
Website URL	
Notes	

Website/Account	
User Name	
Password	
Website URL	
Notes	

Website/Account	
User Name	
Password	
Website URL	
Notes	

Website/Account	
User Name	
Password	
Website URL	
Notes	

Website/Account	
User Name	
Password	
Website URL	
Notes	

Website/Account	
User Name	
Password	
Website URL	
Notes	

K

Website/Account	
User Name	
Password	
Website URL	
Notes	

Website/Account	
User Name	
Password	
Website URL	
Notes	

Website/Account	
User Name	
Password	
Website URL	
Notes	

Website/Account	
User Name	
Password	
Website URL	
Notes	

PASSWORDS and LOG-INS

Website/Account	
User Name	
Password	
Website URL	
Notes	

Website/Account	
User Name	
Password	
Website URL	
Notes	

Website/Account	
User Name	
Password	
Website URL	
Notes	

Website/Account	
User Name	
Password	
Website URL	
Notes	

PASSWORDS and LOG-INS

L

Website/Account	
User Name	
Password	
Website URL	
Notes	

Website/Account	
User Name	
Password	
Website URL	
Notes	

Website/Account	
User Name	
Password	
Website URL	
Notes	

Website/Account	
User Name	
Password	
Website URL	
Notes	

PASSWORDS and LOG-INS

Website/Account	
User Name	
Password	
Website URL	
Notes	

Website/Account	
User Name	
Password	
Website URL	
Notes	

Website/Account	
User Name	
Password	
Website URL	
Notes	

Website/Account	
User Name	
Password	
Website URL	
Notes	

Website/Account	
User Name	
Password	
Website URL	
Notes	

Website/Account	
User Name	
Password	
Website URL	
Notes	

Website/Account	
User Name	
Password	
Website URL	
Notes	

Website/Account	
User Name	
Password	
Website URL	
Notes	

PASSWORDS and LOG-INS

Website/Account	
User Name	
Password	
Website URL	
Notes	

Website/Account	
User Name	
Password	
Website URL	
Notes	

Website/Account	
User Name	
Password	
Website URL	
Notes	

Website/Account	
User Name	
Password	
Website URL	
Notes	

Website/Account	
User Name	
Password	
Website URL	
Notes	

Website/Account	
User Name	
Password	
Website URL	
Notes	

Website/Account	
User Name	
Password	
Website URL	
Notes	

Website/Account	
User Name	
Password	
Website URL	
Notes	

PASSWORDS and LOG-INS

Website/Account	
User Name	
Password	
Website URL	
Notes	

Website/Account	
User Name	
Password	
Website URL	
Notes	

Website/Account	
User Name	
Password	
Website URL	
Notes	

Website/Account	
User Name	
Password	
Website URL	
Notes	

Website/Account	
User Name	
Password	
Website URL	
Notes	

Website/Account	
User Name	
Password	
Website URL	
Notes	

Website/Account	
User Name	
Password	
Website URL	
Notes	

Website/Account	
User Name	
Password	
Website URL	
Notes	

Website/Account	
User Name	
Password	
Website URL	

Notes

Website/Account	
User Name	
Password	
Website URL	

Notes

Website/Account	
User Name	
Password	
Website URL	

Notes

Website/Account	
User Name	
Password	
Website URL	

Notes

N

Website/Account	
User Name	
Password	
Website URL	
Notes	

Website/Account	
User Name	
Password	
Website URL	
Notes	

Website/Account	
User Name	
Password	
Website URL	
Notes	

Website/Account	
User Name	
Password	
Website URL	
Notes	

Website/Account	
User Name	
Password	
Website URL	
Notes	

Website/Account	
User Name	
Password	
Website URL	
Notes	

Website/Account	
User Name	
Password	
Website URL	
Notes	

Website/Account	
User Name	
Password	
Website URL	
Notes	

N

Website/Account	
User Name	
Password	
Website URL	
Notes	

Website/Account	
User Name	
Password	
Website URL	
Notes	

Website/Account	
User Name	
Password	
Website URL	
Notes	

Website/Account	
User Name	
Password	
Website URL	
Notes	

PASSWORDS and LOG-INS

Website/Account	
User Name	
Password	
Website URL	
Notes	

Website/Account	
User Name	
Password	
Website URL	
Notes	

Website/Account	
User Name	
Password	
Website URL	
Notes	

Website/Account	
User Name	
Password	
Website URL	
Notes	

PASSWORDS and LOG-INS

Website/Account	
User Name	
Password	
Website URL	
Notes	

Website/Account	
User Name	
Password	
Website URL	
Notes	

Website/Account	
User Name	
Password	
Website URL	
Notes	

Website/Account	
User Name	
Password	
Website URL	
Notes	

PASSWORDS and LOG-INS

Website/Account	
User Name	
Password	
Website URL	
Notes	

Website/Account	
User Name	
Password	
Website URL	
Notes	

Website/Account	
User Name	
Password	
Website URL	
Notes	

Website/Account	
User Name	
Password	
Website URL	
Notes	

PASSWORDS and LOGINS

Website/Account	
User Name	
Password	
Website URL	
Notes	

Website/Account	
User Name	
Password	
Website URL	
Notes	

Website/Account	
User Name	
Password	
Website URL	
Notes	

Website/Account	
User Name	
Password	
Website URL	
Notes	

Website/Account	
User Name	
Password	
Website URL	

Notes

Website/Account	
User Name	
Password	
Website URL	

Notes

Website/Account	
User Name	
Password	
Website URL	

Notes

Website/Account	
User Name	
Password	
Website URL	

Notes

Website/Account	
User Name	
Password	
Website URL	
Notes	

Website/Account	
User Name	
Password	
Website URL	
Notes	

Website/Account	
User Name	
Password	
Website URL	
Notes	

Website/Account	
User Name	
Password	
Website URL	
Notes	

P PASSWORDS and LOG-INS

Website/Account	
User Name	
Password	
Website URL	
Notes	

Website/Account	
User Name	
Password	
Website URL	
Notes	

Website/Account	
User Name	
Password	
Website URL	
Notes	

Website/Account	
User Name	
Password	
Website URL	
Notes	

Website/Account	
User Name	
Password	
Website URL	
Notes	

Website/Account	
User Name	
Password	
Website URL	
Notes	

Website/Account	
User Name	
Password	
Website URL	
Notes	

Website/Account	
User Name	
Password	
Website URL	
Notes	

PASSWORDS and LOG-INS

Website/Account	
User Name	
Password	
Website URL	
Notes	

Website/Account	
User Name	
Password	
Website URL	
Notes	

Website/Account	
User Name	
Password	
Website URL	
Notes	

Website/Account	
User Name	
Password	
Website URL	
Notes	

Website/Account	
User Name	
Password	
Website URL	
Notes	

Website/Account	
User Name	
Password	
Website URL	
Notes	

Website/Account	
User Name	
Password	
Website URL	
Notes	

Website/Account	
User Name	
Password	
Website URL	
Notes	

Website/Account	
User Name	
Password	
Website URL	
Notes	

Website/Account	
User Name	
Password	
Website URL	
Notes	

Website/Account	
User Name	
Password	
Website URL	
Notes	

Website/Account	
User Name	
Password	
Website URL	
Notes	

PASSWORDS and LOG-INS

R

Website/Account	
User Name	
Password	
Website URL	
Notes	

Website/Account	
User Name	
Password	
Website URL	
Notes	

Website/Account	
User Name	
Password	
Website URL	
Notes	

Website/Account	
User Name	
Password	
Website URL	
Notes	

Website/Account	
User Name	
Password	
Website URL	
Notes	

Website/Account	
User Name	
Password	
Website URL	
Notes	

Website/Account	
User Name	
Password	
Website URL	
Notes	

Website/Account	
User Name	
Password	
Website URL	
Notes	

Website/Account	
User Name	
Password	
Website URL	
Notes	

Website/Account	
User Name	
Password	
Website URL	
Notes	

Website/Account	
User Name	
Password	
Website URL	
Notes	

Website/Account	
User Name	
Password	
Website URL	
Notes	

Website/Account	
User Name	
Password	
Website URL	
Notes	

Website/Account	
User Name	
Password	
Website URL	
Notes	

Website/Account	
User Name	
Password	
Website URL	
Notes	

Website/Account	
User Name	
Password	
Website URL	
Notes	

Website/Account	
User Name	
Password	
Website URL	
Notes	

Website/Account	
User Name	
Password	
Website URL	
Notes	

Website/Account	
User Name	
Password	
Website URL	
Notes	

Website/Account	
User Name	
Password	
Website URL	
Notes	

Website/Account	
User Name	
Password	
Website URL	
Notes	

Website/Account	
User Name	
Password	
Website URL	
Notes	

Website/Account	
User Name	
Password	
Website URL	
Notes	

Website/Account	
User Name	
Password	
Website URL	
Notes	

Website/Account	
User Name	
Password	
Website URL	
Notes	

Website/Account	
User Name	
Password	
Website URL	
Notes	

Website/Account	
User Name	
Password	
Website URL	
Notes	

Website/Account	
User Name	
Password	
Website URL	
Notes	

Website/Account	
User Name	
Password	
Website URL	

Notes

Website/Account	
User Name	
Password	
Website URL	

Notes

Website/Account	
User Name	
Password	
Website URL	

Notes

Website/Account	
User Name	
Password	
Website URL	

Notes

PASSWORDS and LOG-INS

S

Website/Account	
User Name	
Password	
Website URL	
Notes	

Website/Account	
User Name	
Password	
Website URL	
Notes	

Website/Account	
User Name	
Password	
Website URL	
Notes	

Website/Account	
User Name	
Password	
Website URL	
Notes	

Website/Account	
User Name	
Password	
Website URL	
Notes	

Website/Account	
User Name	
Password	
Website URL	
Notes	

Website/Account	
User Name	
Password	
Website URL	
Notes	

Website/Account	
User Name	
Password	
Website URL	
Notes	

S

Website/Account	
User Name	
Password	
Website URL	
Notes	

Website/Account	
User Name	
Password	
Website URL	
Notes	

Website/Account	
User Name	
Password	
Website URL	
Notes	

Website/Account	
User Name	
Password	
Website URL	
Notes	

PASSWORDS and LOG-INS

Website/Account	
User Name	
Password	
Website URL	
Notes	

Website/Account	
User Name	
Password	
Website URL	
Notes	

Website/Account	
User Name	
Password	
Website URL	
Notes	

Website/Account	
User Name	
Password	
Website URL	
Notes	

PASSWORDS and LOG-INS

Website/Account	
User Name	
Password	
Website URL	
Notes	

Website/Account	
User Name	
Password	
Website URL	
Notes	

Website/Account	
User Name	
Password	
Website URL	
Notes	

Website/Account	
User Name	
Password	
Website URL	
Notes	

Website/Account	
User Name	
Password	
Website URL	

Notes

Website/Account	
User Name	
Password	
Website URL	

Notes

Website/Account	
User Name	
Password	
Website URL	

Notes

Website/Account	
User Name	
Password	
Website URL	

Notes

Website/Account	
User Name	
Password	
Website URL	
Notes	

Website/Account	
User Name	
Password	
Website URL	
Notes	

Website/Account	
User Name	
Password	
Website URL	
Notes	

Website/Account	
User Name	
Password	
Website URL	
Notes	

Website/Account	
User Name	
Password	
Website URL	
Notes	

Website/Account	
User Name	
Password	
Website URL	
Notes	

Website/Account	
User Name	
Password	
Website URL	
Notes	

Website/Account	
User Name	
Password	
Website URL	
Notes	

Website/Account	
User Name	
Password	
Website URL	
Notes	

Website/Account	
User Name	
Password	
Website URL	
Notes	

Website/Account	
User Name	
Password	
Website URL	
Notes	

Website/Account	
User Name	
Password	
Website URL	
Notes	

Website/Account	
User Name	
Password	
Website URL	
Notes	

Website/Account	
User Name	
Password	
Website URL	
Notes	

Website/Account	
User Name	
Password	
Website URL	
Notes	

Website/Account	
User Name	
Password	
Website URL	
Notes	

V

Website/Account	
User Name	
Password	
Website URL	
Notes	

Website/Account	
User Name	
Password	
Website URL	
Notes	

Website/Account	
User Name	
Password	
Website URL	
Notes	

Website/Account	
User Name	
Password	
Website URL	
Notes	

Website/Account	
User Name	
Password	
Website URL	
Notes	

Website/Account	
User Name	
Password	
Website URL	
Notes	

Website/Account	
User Name	
Password	
Website URL	
Notes	

Website/Account	
User Name	
Password	
Website URL	
Notes	

Website/Account	
User Name	
Password	
Website URL	
Notes	

Website/Account	
User Name	
Password	
Website URL	
Notes	

Website/Account	
User Name	
Password	
Website URL	
Notes	

Website/Account	
User Name	
Password	
Website URL	
Notes	

Website/Account	
User Name	
Password	
Website URL	
Notes	

Website/Account	
User Name	
Password	
Website URL	
Notes	

Website/Account	
User Name	
Password	
Website URL	
Notes	

Website/Account	
User Name	
Password	
Website URL	
Notes	

PASSWORDS and LOG-INS

W

Website/Account	
User Name	
Password	
Website URL	
Notes	

Website/Account	
User Name	
Password	
Website URL	
Notes	

Website/Account	
User Name	
Password	
Website URL	
Notes	

Website/Account	
User Name	
Password	
Website URL	
Notes	

Website/Account	
User Name	
Password	
Website URL	
Notes	

Website/Account	
User Name	
Password	
Website URL	
Notes	

Website/Account	
User Name	
Password	
Website URL	
Notes	

Website/Account	
User Name	
Password	
Website URL	
Notes	

PASSWORDS and LOG-INS

W

Website/Account	
User Name	
Password	
Website URL	
Notes	

Website/Account	
User Name	
Password	
Website URL	
Notes	

Website/Account	
User Name	
Password	
Website URL	
Notes	

Website/Account	
User Name	
Password	
Website URL	
Notes	

Website/Account	
User Name	
Password	
Website URL	
Notes	

Website/Account	
User Name	
Password	
Website URL	
Notes	

Website/Account	
User Name	
Password	
Website URL	
Notes	

Website/Account	
User Name	
Password	
Website URL	
Notes	

W

Website/Account	
User Name	
Password	
Website URL	
Notes	

Website/Account	
User Name	
Password	
Website URL	
Notes	

Website/Account	
User Name	
Password	
Website URL	
Notes	

Website/Account	
User Name	
Password	
Website URL	
Notes	

Website/Account	
User Name	
Password	
Website URL	
Notes	

Website/Account	
User Name	
Password	
Website URL	
Notes	

Website/Account	
User Name	
Password	
Website URL	
Notes	

Website/Account	
User Name	
Password	
Website URL	
Notes	

PASSWORDS and LOGINS

Website/Account	
User Name	
Password	
Website URL	
Notes	

Website/Account	
User Name	
Password	
Website URL	
Notes	

Website/Account	
User Name	
Password	
Website URL	
Notes	

Website/Account	
User Name	
Password	
Website URL	
Notes	

Website/Account	
User Name	
Password	
Website URL	
Notes	

Website/Account	
User Name	
Password	
Website URL	
Notes	

Website/Account	
User Name	
Password	
Website URL	
Notes	

Website/Account	
User Name	
Password	
Website URL	
Notes	

PASSWORDS and LOG-INS

Y

Website/Account	
User Name	
Password	
Website URL	
Notes	

Website/Account	
User Name	
Password	
Website URL	
Notes	

Website/Account	
User Name	
Password	
Website URL	
Notes	

Website/Account	
User Name	
Password	
Website URL	
Notes	

Website/Account	
User Name	
Password	
Website URL	
Notes	

Website/Account	
User Name	
Password	
Website URL	
Notes	

Website/Account	
User Name	
Password	
Website URL	
Notes	

Website/Account	
User Name	
Password	
Website URL	
Notes	

Website/Account	
User Name	
Password	
Website URL	
Notes	

Website/Account	
User Name	
Password	
Website URL	
Notes	

Website/Account	
User Name	
Password	
Website URL	
Notes	

Website/Account	
User Name	
Password	
Website URL	
Notes	

WI-FI and ROUTER LOG-INS

Network/SSID	
Password	
Encryption	

Notes:

Network/SSID	
Password	
Encryption	

Notes:

Network/SSID	
Password	
Encryption	

Notes:

Network/SSID	
Password	
Encryption	

Notes:

SOFTWARE LICENSES

Software Name		Version	
Key/Serial #			
Licensed To			
Download URL			
Support			
Date Purchased		Price	
Notes:			

Software Name		Version	
Key/Serial #			
Licensed To			
Download URL			
Support			
Date Purchased		Price	
Notes:			

Software Name		Version	
Key/Serial #			
Licensed To			
Download URL			
Support			
Date Purchased		Price	
Notes:			

SOFTWARE LICENSES

Software Name		Version	
Key/Serial #			
Licensed To			
Download URL			
Support			
Date Purchased		Price	

Notes:

Software Name		Version	
Key/Serial #			
Licensed To			
Download URL			
Support			
Date Purchased		Price	

Notes:

Software Name		Version	
Key/Serial #			
Licensed To			
Download URL			
Support			
Date Purchased		Price	

Notes:

SOFTWARE LICENSES

Software Name		Version	
Key/Serial #			
Licensed To			
Download URL			
Support			
Date Purchased		Price	
Notes:			

Software Name		Version	
Key/Serial #			
Licensed To			
Download URL			
Support			
Date Purchased		Price	
Notes:			

Software Name		Version	
Key/Serial #			
Licensed To			
Download URL			
Support			
Date Purchased		Price	
Notes:			

SOFTWARE LICENSES

Software Name		Version	
Key/Serial #			
Licensed To			
Download URL			
Support			
Date Purchased		Price	
Notes:			

Software Name		Version	
Key/Serial #			
Licensed To			
Download URL			
Support			
Date Purchased		Price	
Notes:			

Software Name		Version	
Key/Serial #			
Licensed To			
Download URL			
Support			
Date Purchased		Price	
Notes:			

www.ingramcontent.com/pod-product-compliance
Lightning Source LLC
Chambersburg PA
CBHW071300050326
40690CB00011B/2478